Khoji Ahmar

YULDUZKHAN AHMAR

KHOJI AHMAR

iUniverse books may be ordered through booksellers or by contacting:

iUniverse
1663 Liberty Drive
Bloomington, IN 47403
www.iuniverse.com
844-349-9409

Because of the dynamic nature of the internet, any web addresses or links contained in this book may have changed since publication and may no longer be valid. The views expressed in this work are solely those of the author and do not necessarily reflect the views of the publisher, and the publisher hereby disclaims any responsibility for them.

Any people depicted in stock imagery provided by Getty Images are models, and such images are being used for illustrative purposes only.
Certain stock imagery © Getty Images.

ISBN: 978-1-5320-9326-5 (sc)
ISBN: 978-1-5320-9324-1 (hc)
ISBN: 978-1-5320-9325-8 (e)

Library of Congress Control Number: 2021909181

Print information available on the last page.

iUniverse rev. date: 10/20/2021

The drop of water reflects the world in all its glory.
—Kh. Ahmar

I wrote this book to record my memories of the members of our large family, those still living and those who are no longer among us—my favorite uncle, Khoji Ahmar; my beloved father, Mirodil Akhmerov; and all my ancestors. I have the utmost respect and appreciation for them, and I hope they will abide in our memories forever.

We obtain satisfaction when we overcome obstacles and difficulties in our lives; we obtain it when we find a path that leads to the answers to all our questions, which benefits us and others in our daily actions and whatever occupations we are engaged in.

Contents

Introduction

I wrote this book about a talented person, a multifaceted personality, a director, writer, linguist, screenwriter, actor, and artist—Khoji Ahmar. His work was permeated with his humanism and love for his homeland, and he shared his love with society, the world, and nature. His works clearly portray his commitment to excellence, his tireless work to achieve his goals, and the diligent progress he has made toward achieving them.

Some of his successful films are *Hard Way*, *The Swallows Arrive in Spring*, *Four Seasons of the Year*, *Integral*, and *Satellite of the Planet Uranus*.

One of the best films in the republic of Uzbekistan, *Daughter of the Ganges*, played a special role in Ahmar's life, as he produced this film as well. The following works of Ahmar's are documentaries: *At Don Breeders*, *Cooperative Sanatorium*, *My Dear Moscovites*, and a popular science film, *Songs of Tamarahanum*. He wrote the script for the animated movies *Traditions of Centuries*, *Next on the Ground*, and *Most Obedient*.

He translated Russian classics into the Uzbek language, including *The Stone Guest* by Alexander Pushkin, *Bearers* by Oles Gonchar, *Great Family* together with writer Khamid Gulyam, and *Sergei Bondarchuk*, which he wrote but was not published.

In 2017, the movies *Daughter of Ganges* and *Integral* were awarded the "Gold Found" of Republic Uzbekistan's movie industry.

He was a creator who was proud of his work ethic and the sweet fruits of his labor. Ever since he was a child, he loved nature, starry skies, and animals. He appreciated the primordial and natural beauty in every aspect of the world. This made him optimistic about life, and he continued to distribute the beauty he saw to other people in his work.

In all his work, he affirmed his desire to be in harmony with the world. My father, Mirodil, Ahmar's older brother, encapsulated Ahmar's belief in a brief phrase: "Life—a wonderful gift of nature." Ahmar learned that for life to bring him joy, he needed to work with passion and love.

Each person has a favorite place on earth, a color, a meal, and an animal. Uncle Khoji and my father chose blue—they were always attracted to the sea—and green—they loved grassy hills. They spent their childhoods in a mountainous area.

Our Family

My Grandpa Miftah, Grandma Gulasal Ayajon
and Dad Miradil

One of our great-grandparents, Ahmar Domla, was a teacher and farmer. The feudal system and Khan's regime taught literacy to young adults who wanted to be educated.

He and his wife, our great-grandmother Tursunoi Aya, raised literate and hardworking children. They were taught to be formal and always helpful to people. They were the roots of the family. The successors were Mullah Miftah and Gulasal Aya Akhmerova.

Mullah Miftah was a tall, slender, and handsome man. He was strict, clever, and competent, and he loved his family and children. Most people respected him; his family took his advice and suggestions, and neighbors often turned to him for advice. He was very passionate and friendly, and he was always smiling. Dadajon (grandfather), was always positively involved in our lives; he told us stories and guided us in life.

His wife, Gulasal Ayajon, was beautiful; she had strawberry-red cheeks and was a sweet and gentle woman. She was very hospitable; she loved and welcomed everyone who visited her. She respected all types of labor and taught that ethic to the children in her life. She loved to tell us fairy tales at bedtime that included songs and jokes; they were very long tales, and we would fall asleep during them, but we couldn't wait for the next night to hear more of her tales; some took her a week of nights to finish. She was respectfully submissive to her husband, but she made sure that her children and grandchildren were under her protective wings.

My father, Mirodil Akhmerov (to whom elderly people refer as Eshon-Aka later on for respect), was the eldest son in his family. He was born on February 17, 1925. He had a strong spirit; he was well built but also gentle, and he was very intelligent. He was soft spoken and had wavy hair and handsome features. He was always dressed in a classic style. He was respected and loved by all others, who were attracted by his positive energy. He served in high positions in Internal Affairs enforcement. He was very responsible, and he demanded punctuality from those who worked for him.

He loved to joke. He kept a good mood aura, and he had a friendly energy among others. He was into sports; he was a big fan of the soccer/football team Pakhtakor and did not miss a game. Yuri Pshenichnikov, the team's goalkeeper, lived in the next apartment complex from us, and they would often catch up with conversations. He mourned the tragic death of his favorite team members.

He had a great collection of books written by Ferdowsi, Nizami, Alisher Navoi, Abdulla Kadiri, Erkin Vakhidov, Aybek, and others, along with Shakespeare's plays, Jack London, and Theodore Dreiser. Among his favorite writers were Leo Tolstoy, Nikolai Nekrasov, and Fyodor Dostoevsky.

His vast knowledge and many life experiences taught him right from wrong and made him able to make good decisions and advise others. He kept his family safe, and he exhibited his personal greatness.

This reminds me of some wise words.

> Life seems meaningless until you fall in love, and only love gives it its meaning. It's love in our lives that gives us passion towards something, which makes us reach some goals. Because of love every moment of our life becomes valuable. A person that queries, "What is the meaning

of life" is lacking love. When one loves, he never asks what the meaning of life is and doesn't need to ask of the meaning, as the meaning of life is love. (Osho)

Khizirulla Akhmerov, born on February 18, 1929, was the second son of the family. He looked strict, but he was very kind and loving toward his parents, brothers, and sisters. He was always his brother's faithful friend and companion. After him came their younger brother, Kudrat Aka, and sisters Mukarramhon and Muazzamhon.

Grandpa Mullah Miftah (Mulla is a title given to educated people) and Gulasalhon Aya were very kind. They taught their children to be honest and fair; they showed them the true meaning of love and shared with them their desire to protect nature and appreciate natural beauty. They taught their children to respect themselves and others, to never lie, to honor their elders, and to respect their home by helping out with chores.

We had a spacious yard and a garden in which we grew apricots, apples, cherries, figs, and grapes. We raised many animals, including horses, cows, goats, rams, hens, ducks, geese, and turkeys. Mujic, our dog, was always running around, and we had a cat named Vaska.

Everyone in the family stayed busy, but the children had time to read, play games, and engage their curiosity. All the work and play taught the family to be honest and fair.

The family experienced the deaths of five of their ten children, so Grandpa's strictness and discipline were out of love for his children. He explained the basics of life and often reminded the words of Omar Khayyam.

We are the source of fun—and sorrow mine,
We receptacle of filth and pure spring.
Man, as if in a mirror peaceful multifaceted,
He is worthless—and he is infinitely great!

It does not matter—from what you will die,
It is much more important—for what are … you were born.

Childhood

In the Uzun kucha neighborhood of Bostanlik, a village, you could hear children's loud voices and watch boys playing soccer and being cheered on by spectators at their games. Children played tag or *chillak*, a bowling game.

In the spring, kids made kites and competed with each other to see whose could fly the highest and stay up the longest. In the summer, they swam in the river. In the fall, they harvested grapes, corn, apples, apricots, and cherries.

Khoji Aka attended the local school with his older brother Mirodil. Kumush Rasultaev, who taught for more than forty years in the village, remembered every student whom he had ever taught. He remembered Mirodil and Khizirullah as highly capable pupils who aced their classes from the first grade on. The family then moved to Tashkent mahalla, Rabochiy gorodok, where the boys graduated from high school.

The family reminisces about life in the mountains and relatives there. My brothers remember Uncle Normat Aka, who gave Mirodil and Khizirulla flatbread. He was glad to see that the children were on the path to building bright futures, but the separation upset him.

In the village, Uncle Normat Aka was a very respected man. He was tall and athletic, and he worked as a blacksmith. He was able to repair anything from tractors and wristwatches to samovars (pots for boiling tea) and women's earrings.

During school holidays, the children would leave the mountains in their native village.

Summer

One day, Gulasal Ayajon visited her brother, Turajan. Ayajon, who was famous for being hospitable to everyone who visited her, would cook very delicious *pilaf,* a rice dish. She would push plates toward her guests and say, "Olin, Olin!" ("Help yourself!")

The adults would sit on couches in the courtyard while the children frolicked. Uncle Turajan got Miftah daddy's permission to take the children on a vacation to Pargos, a village where many of Gulasal Ayajon's relatives, including her brothers and sisters, lived.

In those days, the roofs of homes were flat; at harvest time, people dried grapes, apples, apricots, melons, and tomatoes on them. Mirodil, Khizirulla, and their cousins played together. All the kids liked the sky and the stars; they loved to sleep on the couch in the courtyard or on the roof. Looking at the sky, they talked about their childhood experiences and debated about which stars shined the brightest and how far away they were. They had dreams of the future as do all children.

Little Mirodil loved horses, and he cared for them, brushed them, and talked to them. At home, he had his own horses that he cared for. At Uncle Turajan's house, when the adults came home from work, they allowed him to ride. When the dog gave birth to puppies, the children cared for them. Four puppies had dark fur while a fifth was a light brown with a small spot on his forehead. Khizirulla loved playing with it; he would feed him before he sat down to eat himself.

When it was time to go home, Uncle Turajan gave the puppy to him. On the way home, the puppy unexpectedly jumped out of the bus and ran. At first, the children were confused, but then they chased it and found it drinking from a stream. They got back on the bus and got home without further incident. Khizirulla Aka named his new pet Mujik. It was a German shepherd, which grew large and lived with us for a long time.

Later, another child was born—my uncle Kudrat. The older guys were very excited and told everyone about it, and they even wrote on the schoolyard wall that they had a little brother. Later, when Kudrat started attending school, his older brothers showed him the inscription.

Gulasal Aya doted on the children, and their grandfather engaged them from an early age by telling them stories and fairy tales and teaching them to read and write. The children became very friendly with each other and always helped and loved each other.

Adult Children

Time passed quickly. The children were growing, and their parents thought about their future. Dadajon Mullah Miftah knew how to identify and encourage the children's abilities. In the postwar period, many people saw a bright future. Parents wanted their children to be highly educated and proud of their success and achievements. Dadajon Mullah Miftah was always a wise counselor. He closely followed their progress in life; he knew the abilities and aspirations of each of them. He understood that in order to overcome life's difficulties, they needed to work hard.

To become professional at anything requires persistence and insistence. If you are lucky to have talents and are willing to work hard, you can become a creator, a rare combination of talents, and work at school and beyond. Dadajon never went contrary to the wishes of the children; he always took their personal interests into consideration.

After they graduated from high school, the boys and girls went to college. After my father completed studies at a Tashkent officers' school, he entered the military academy in Moscow.

Khizirulla Aka successfully passed the exams in the faculty of the history of the Persian language at Tashkent State University.

Kudrat Aka became a scientist, a professor with an academic degree, in 2018, and working in Polytechnic University. He had a passion for gardening; he cultivated new varieties of grapes and fruit trees. His wife, Gulya Opa, a dentist, was the mother of four children, and she had grandchildren and great-grandchildren.

Mukarramhon Opa also graduated from Tashkent State University; she became a journalist and worked in the publishing house Fan at the Academy of Sciences of the Uzbek SSR. Her husband, Khaybatulla Aliev, a Uzbek TV employee, was a talented filmmaker. They had four children and many grandchildren.

Muazzamhon Opa followed her ancestors; she graduated from the Department of the Oriental Institute History of the Persian language and taught at the school. I spoke with some of her former pupils, who spoke about her with respect and with love. Muazzamhon Opa had a deep and abiding interest in teaching. Her husband, Sabirjan Yodgorov, worked at the Tashkent Medical Institute and contributed greatly to the development of the health system by utilizing the latest medical equipment. They have three children and many grandchildren.

Portrait of Khoji Ahmar

Khoji Ahmar

Khizirulla Akhmerov was tall; his black hair was straight and stubborn. His forehead was broad and slightly elongated, and his eyes were dark and expressive. He was quite strict as the head of his family. He was a man of few words, but he always expressed himself clearly. He was proud of his name and the success of his friends and relatives.

He loved children. He was always direct and truthful and told people what he thought. Many people he dealt with could not take that, and it led to conflicts with colleagues at work. My father constantly asked him to be more diplomatic when dealing with others. Khoji Aka often repeated the conversational word *yomasam*, which corresponds to the indefinite "so-so." That allowed him to focus and give a reasoned response. His feedback was much appreciated, and no one dared to speak to him about everything and nothing. He was attentive to all without exception.

The brothers valued beauty very highly, but in some cases, their opinions diverged. If Uncle found fault with women for using cosmetics saying that natural beauty was more important, my father would say that it was okay to help nature along.

Khoji Aka spent much time with his family; he often worked with the children, but he also spoiled them a little. Our parents did not spoil us, and they were strict. My father was always busy at work or on business trips, but he did engage with us.

As a journalist at *Kizil Uzbekiston*, a newspaper, Khoji Ahmar was familiar with many of the leaders of the republic. He could go directly to the secretary of the Central Committee of the Communist Party of Uzbekistan, Sharaf Rashidovich Rashidov, or to Prime Minister Yodgor Nasreddinova. Many of his friends and acquaintances have become major, long-term leaders, prominent figures of science and culture.

While in Moscow and Kiev on business, he met a young Russian girl and decided to marry her. Dadajon did not agree, but the decisive Khoji Aka did not retreat; he met with Prime Minister Yodgor Nasreddinova and brought her home. She had a long chat with his father, and Miftah Dadajon did not stand in the way of their marriage.

They married, and Lyudmila Ivanovna Tolstopyatova became a member of our big family. She was a very sweet, friendly, and respectable woman, and she quickly learned the language. I was five at that time, and I heard my parents talk about her approvingly. Lyudahon Opa (her name in Uzbek) would put me on her lap and read Russian folk tales to me, and she taught me to read Russian. She told me about Russian dishes, and I told her about Uzbek food and particularly what I liked. It was a very good topic of conversation for two people of different ages and languages, and we became close. She was a librarian; she loved books as much as her husband did. Most likely, that was what had attracted them to each other. She became a friend and his assistant. They have two children and many grandchildren.

My uncle was a man of peace and goodwill who helped everyone he could. Auntie Mukarramhon Opa said that when she and her friends wanted to go to the movies, Khoji Aka would give them money for the tickets and more for ice cream.

Khoji Aka loved working. He locked himself at home, smoked a lot, and did not communicate for a time with anyone. Without rest, he wrote stories and drew portraits and views. Even when he rested, he tried to be useful somehow. He was a great cook and loved to eat delicious food.

The Generosity of Kind People

In 1966, a catastrophic earthquake occurred in Tashkent. Many buildings were destroyed; one-story houses just disappeared. People were afraid that high-rise buildings, whose walls and ceilings were cracked, might collapse as well. The aftershocks lasted for days and caused more destruction. All the great Soviet countries came to the aid of Uzbekistan. Rescuers, medical workers, and construction crews came from fifteen union republics, as did many of our neighbors who lived in high-rise buildings near the military base, where we lived in the courtyard.

It was during those difficult days in 1966 that Dadajon was appointed to arrange the wedding of my sister; my father was on a business trip. Grandpa, as the head of a large family, wanted to celebrate the wedding after my father returned, but he was detained. Young Khoji Aka decided to help his brother's family and promptly organized the event. With the help of soldiers from the military base, he set up tables, chairs, and everything else needed for the ceremony in the courtyard of our apartment complex. It was an unusual but very fun wedding for all who attended, including the children.

My sister and her husband lived a happy and dignified life. They had five children and have many grandchildren. I am very grateful for everything Khoji Aka did for my beloved sister; he made many people very happy. He never boasted about the assistance he had provided; that was typical of him.

Portrait of Mirodil Akhmerov

Miradil Ahmerov

Mirodil Akhmerov, born February 17, 1925, was the first child in the family and set the tone. Experience shows that in many families much depends on the upbringing of the older children, who help raise their younger siblings.

Mirodil was of medium height; he had dark eyes, dark, wavy hair, and pleasant features. By nature, he was strict, tactful, and fair, and he spoke calmly and quietly. He was curious, determined, very pleasant to communicate with, and witty. He was always well-groomed. He loved order in the family, and he made decisions and stood firm on them. We kids always asked him about something only once knowing that we could not change his decisions. Our house had military discipline.

Throughout his life, Mirodil worked hard and with dignity. He thought through all the details and never abused his power, but he was demanding of himself and his subordinates.

Mirodil was repeatedly awarded orders and medals of the Republic of Uzbekistan. One high award was presented to him by the secretary of the Central Committee of the Communist Party of the Uzbek SSR, Sh. R. Rashidov. His award read, "For services such as courage in maintaining public order before the Motherland and the people—Sh. R. Rashidov."

His merits were recognized outside the Republic of Uzbekistan. The USSR Ministry of Defense noted him "for valor and courage during World War II." He was awarded a medal by the minister of defense of the USSR and marshal of the Soviet Union, A. Grechko.

He was objective and very literate. He was benevolent toward everyone, including strangers. My father read a lot, had a large library, and loved many writers including Firdowsi and Omar Khayyam, who wrote,

> To be beautiful, does not mean it will be born,
> After to be a beauty we can learn,
> When the soul is beautiful person,
> What looks can be compared with it?

He loved life; he liked singing songs from the play *Tahir and Zuhra*, in which an honored artist of the republic Mahmudjon Gofurov performed. His favorite song was "Hey Kuyosh" ("Sunshine"). Despite the severity, he remained a favorite, good dad who always supported us and gave us his best advice. Thanks to him, we gained a very strong and solid foundation of knowledge. He was a beloved father, teacher, mentor, best friend, colleague, and advisor in many life and service issues. I know many wonderful people, but I have never met anyone with such a beautiful soul. He never denied those who turned to him for advice, and he was always very protective of his family. He was a loving father, a loving brother, our favorite dad, and our children's favorite dadajon. The brothers loved their family and were proud of their names and surname; that was something Dadajon always stressed.

My father's friends and colleagues often came to our house to celebrate birthdays, have feasts, commemorate office successes, and during holidays. We were always drawn together when we were enjoying such events. My parents always said that the more often relatives met for dinner, the warmer their hearts would become. There was amazing mutual affection and communication between the brothers.

If the company we entertained at any time did not include Khoji Aka, my father would become upset. The brothers often talked heart to heart about family issues and always found solutions acceptable to all. They also talked about art, literature, news, science, and technology.

Portrait of Kudrat Akhmerov

Kudrat Ahmerov

Kudrat Akhmerovich Akhmerov, born August 2, 1937, in Tashkent, was the third child in the family. He was of medium height and had a very fair complexion, which caused his brothers to call him Sari Aka, "light brother." He combed his light-brown hair back. He was naturally persistent, diligent, and calm. He dressed neatly—always in a suit and tie.

After high school, he entered the chemical engineering department at Tashkent Polytechnic Institute. After graduating, he worked at the Department of Organic Chemistry. He enrolled in graduate school at Moscow Lomonosov State University, and in 1966, he defended his scientific degree: Candidate Technicheskih Nauk.

He returned to Tashkent and was a senior lecturer and then the senior lecturer in the Department of Organic Chemistry at the Polytechnic Institute. In 1969, he was appointed deputy dean of the Faculty of Chemical Technology and worked in this position until 1983 while teaching students of chemistry and technology.

In 1981, Kudrat defended his doctoral thesis at the Moscow Academy of Thin Fibers. He had discovered a new chemical reaction that was subsequently named, at the suggestion of Professor O. N. Temkin, the "Reaction of Akhmerov."

Later, when he worked at the Moscow Institute of Organic Chemistry, he participated in the development of new technological processes that were successfully implemented in the practice of many domestic chemical enterprises. His proposed new technology was awarded a medal at the Exhibition of National Economy of the Republic of Uzbekistan.

He published two monographs, and under his tutelage three students earned doctorates and eight earned master's degrees.

Professor Akhmerov is a member of the Union of Journalists of Uzbekistan, a famous source of scientific knowledge that the chemical industry relies on. He writes for many magazines and journals including *Chemistry and Life*, *Gulhan*, *Ogonyok*, *Sirli Olam—Mysterious World*, and *Polytechnic*, a newspaper. He actively participates in congresses named after D. I. Mendeleev and the Knowledge society. As a mentor, counselor, and director of research, he organized the Olympiad for students and gives them themes for scientific research.

In the house, we always find him at work reading or writing. Kudrat Aka is a great conversationalist who expresses his thoughts and opinions clearly. In his rare moments of relaxation, he is in the yard or garden working with seedlings that ultimately produce grapes.

Kudrat Aka still has youthful enthusiasm, the result of his constant communication with youth. Maybe it's in his blood.

Portrait of Khaybatulla Aliev

Tashkent, TV bilding. 1969.
Khaybatulla Aliev with his son.

Khaybatulla Aliev, born May 1, 1934, into the family of Ali Eshon and Muazzamhon Aya, is the only son among five children. The kids respected each other, and their mother was kind. I note here the friendship of our two grandmothers, Gulasal Ayajon and Muazzamhon Ayajon, who were like twin sisters. They always went together on holidays to visit relatives.

Khaybatulla Aliev was tall and had dark hair, dark eyes, plump lips, and a ready smile. He supported and encouraged others, and he was very kind. He was an upright, fair-minded, honest, curious, and active organizer—an interesting young man. He was a talented director and writer of TV shows. On national television, he directed and edited musical and theatrical programs. His talent, initiative, merit, and knowledge of theater were evident in more than two hundred dramas. He received the cooperation of Gayrat Ubaydullaev and Hamid Kahramonov. Some of the works of Khaybatulla Aliev took pride of place in the golden fund of cinematography and television productions of the country. The channels Madaniyat wa marifat, Culture and Knowledge, and Cinema periodically broadcast the dramas.

"Khaybatulla Aliev's work is of great importance for the preservation and transmission of role performance art on stage talented, unique actors and is a school for the younger generation," said honored art worker of the Republic of Uzbekistan Mahkam Muhamedov in his article "The Second Life Performances." Performances such as *Maysara's Tricks*, *Riot Brides*, *Emigrants*, *Robot-wife*, and *Travel to Tashkent* remain favorites of viewers particularly when they featured unique actors such as Zainab Sadrieva, Razzaq Khamraev, and Ikroma Boltaeva.

One of his most famous productions was *Abadiyat qonuni* (*Law of Eternity*), which was based on the Georgian writer Nodar Dumbadze's novel. The following reflects the main idea of the play.

> The soul of man is a hundred times heavier than his body … It is so heavy that one person cannot bear it … And because we, the people, still alive, must try help each other, to try to immortalize each other's soul, for example: you—mine, and I—the other, the other—the third and so on to infinity … in order to a person's death is not doomed us to be alone in life.

Khaybatulla often hosted writers, satirists, theater and movie actors, singers, and other artists. Residents of his *mahalla* (housing complex) and relatives respected and loved him. I often visited them at home and saw how hard he worked on scripts for television productions and coaching actors for their roles. He and the writer Said Akhmad created a script based on the novel *The Last Bullet*. He also worked on the production of television dramas including *Do You Miss the Spring?*, *Horizon*, and *Moth*. He spent a lot of time in the library and worked tirelessly. He achieved great success in his career and was a well-deserved authority among colleagues and friends.

Student Years of Khizirulla Akhmerov

After graduating from high school in 1946, Khizirulla Akhmerov entered the Faculty of Oriental Studies at Tashkent State University to study the history of the Middle East. In his third year, Kissen Ilya Albertovich, a linguist, demanded that the students gain knowledge of their native languages and chided them for not being able to properly express their thoughts in their native languages. Khoji Aka spoke Uzbek and Russian very well, but the teacher insisted. Khoji persisted, and as proof of his knowledge of the native language, he translated *Bearers*, a book written by Oles Gonchar.

He wrote and published several of stories under the pseudonym Khoji Ahmar. Since then, he has been known by that name. He also wrote in Russian, Farsi, and Arabic (which he studied independently). After graduating from the university, he worked as a journalist for the newspaper *Kizil Uzbekiston* as well as on the radio. He read the stories of Leo Tolstoy several times. He listened to his inner voice and thought about what he read.

Khoji Aka was tall, as was his father, and many paid attention to him. Gulasal Ayajon told Dadajon that it was time for his son to marry; many women who lived in the mahalla had their eyes locked on him, and Gulasal Aya liked one in particular. My grandfather agreed with Gulasal Aya's choice in that matter, but Khoji said that it was not time for him to marry; he was very busy with other things.

At the end of the 1940s, many Asian and African countries gained independence, and among them was India. The Soviet Union strongly supported India's independence and developed friendly scientific and cultural ties with the country. During that time, many Indian directors produced famous films including Raj Kapoor (*Awaara* and *Mister-420*), Mehboob Khan (*Mother India*), and Vijay Bhatt (*Baiju Bawra*). These movies made a deep impression on many. Everyone enjoyed singing the song "Awaarahum" from the film *Awaara*.

I have always loved Indian films. Many times, I tried to persuade Aunt Mukarramhon Opa, her mother-in-law Muazzamhon Ayajon, and grandmother Gulasal Ayajon to come with me in the summer to the Shukhrat cinema, which was close to our home at the time. We also enjoyed watching TV shows, which featured songs from Indian movies.

One day, when I was eleven or twelve, my father and I watched a concert on TV. He told me that Indian movies had influenced Uncle Khoji; they had awakened his heart and mind, and an inner voice told him what he should devote his life to. The writer and journalist realized that his true calling was to become a filmmaker.

At the time, his brothers were in Moscow; Dad Mirodil was studying at the military academy, and Kudrat Aka had graduated from Moscow State University, but Khoji's parents were concerned about his decision to go to Moscow. However, he was determined to go, leaving Miftah Dadajon to take care of the family.

Here's what Khoji said about the entrance examination he took to enter the All-Union State Institute of Film Studies.

> The long dark corridor, crowded with applicants, all in fear and excitement sat as they saw the chairman of the selection committee, and next to him was a gray-haired man with a cane—as it turned out, it was Alexander Dovzhenko. The selection committee has started and called names. He came out to the corridor very upset, and said that he most likely failed. It turns out that after a brief while Dovzhenko asked what his profession was, and learned that the man was a fisherman and asked him, "So how is it better to fish—using a fishing rod or a net?" The

commission members and a student were arguing, no one coming to a negotiation, and thought he failed the exam. As it turned out, he was wrong: he was accepted and later he became quite the successful filmmaker.

One of the examiners took my uncle and another entrant into the free audience and asked them to sketch Axinya's death (*The Quiet Don* by Sholokhov). On the sheet of paper he put, "It was evening, the sunset."

My uncle remembered that the applicant next to him immediately answered all the test questions while he did not know where to start, but he began creating some dialogue and completed a script, which ended with, "Farewell, Ksyusha!"

He collected his things and prepared to leave, but he was summoned by the selection committee. He read monologues in Russian and Uzbek as well as his first script. So in 1955, Khoji Ahmar was enrolled in the directing group of Professor A. P. Dovzhenko's All-Union State Institute of film studies (VGIK).

The Teacher

Kh. Ahmar loved and respected Alexander Petrovich Dovzhenko, his teacher. He considered his films to be great contributions to cinema. The teacher did not say much about technique, scenes, and perspective; instead, he emphasized the philosophical aspect of creativity. He said, "Art is a set of truth and beauty, which complement each other."

When Dovzhenko spoke about beauty, he would elaborate on the creativity of the writer Anatole France, who saw beauty in truth. He repeatedly talked to students about dialogue with the famous painter Courbet and a fashionable woman.

"Mr. Courbet, when you create a picture, what do you think?"

"I do not think of anything, madame!"

"Really? How is that?"

"I am always too excited when I create!"

Dovzhenko had a parable about two people stepping over a puddle on the street; one saw the mud and slush in it while the other was fascinated by the stars that the puddle was reflecting. He taught future filmmakers to see life through the work of only luminous stars. Dovzhenko argued that the work of a filmmaker was not to be trifled with; he did not have patience for inattention or indifference.

Dovzhenko helped create a park at the entrance to the studio Mosfilm in Kiev after he walked around the area and saw discarded building materials and trash. He stopped all normal activities at the studio for a few days and organized a team and bulldozers and tractors to transform the area into a park, complete with fruit trees and flowers. It was a beautiful place that delighted all who visited the studio.

One day, Khoji Aka and Dovzhenko were looking out the window of the studio and admiring the park when they saw two young directors walking in the park.

"I wonder what they are talking about," the professor said. "Let's go and ask them."

They went out and approached the two men, and the professor asked, "Hello, guys. What have you been talking about?"

"Nothing really," one said.

"Look around. What do you see?" the professor asked.

They looked around, shrugged, and said, "Nothing."

"Young men," the professor said, "you have chosen the wrong profession."

Dovzhenko spoke to a friend of his, Krylov, a famous mathematician and academician, about people's indifference and irresponsibility. The academician lived on the ground floor of an old and famous high-rise in Moscow; the windows of his office looked out on the courtyard. One time, the noise that children in the courtyard were making as they played became too much, so he went outside and told the children to quiet down. A girl asked him, "Why are you scolding us? If you're frustrated, why don't you teach us how to behave?" The academician realized that at other times, he had been indifferent to the noise the children made, and he decided to keep on being indifferent to it.

Professor Olga Alexandrovna Yakubovskaya taught at K. S. Stanislavskogo, an acting institution. The professor gave the example of works by Alexander Fadeyev, such as *Young Guard*. In one episode, before the cowardly soldier shot the enemy, he turned a blind eye, but no one was paying attention. The lesson in that episode was, "Here begins betrayal."

Dovzhenko was very attentive to his students. When he entered the classroom, he would look at each student and ask some, "You're not looking good today. Is something wrong? Maybe you're tired?" Indeed, many students had to work and on weekends as well. Addressing the students, he told them, "The meaning of life is to work, so do not think it will become easier."

The professor took all his students on a guided tour of the Moscow area to visit Peredelkino Horvino, Abramtsevo, Vladimir, Suzdal, and Klin to explore the historic sites and museums. When a student said that it would require a bus, Dovzhenko said that he would soon receive payment for a screenplay of the film *Poem of the Sea* that would handle that expense.

Alexander Petrovich talked with the pupils about sports and about the dangers of smoking. He had smoked for fifteen years but had rid himself of that bad habit. He insisted that directors should stay strong and healthy and at the same time sensual.

Sometimes his judgments seemed unexpected. He said that singers needed to know how to sing, those who designed and built sets had to be creative, and actors had to know their craft, but directors could be without talent as long as they were philosophers with good hearts. He felt that directors must be able to review each frame of a film with their souls, that they had to live for the day, for the next day, and for the future, and that they had to be creative or their work would quickly die.

In his notes, my uncle recorded his words uttered in 1956, the year of "Here I am living the dream of the 1960th year." He foresaw the launching of space rockets. Then, it seemed like a fantasy, a pipe dream, but it was reality within five years!

After watching the film *41st*, Alexander Petrovich asked the students what they noticed. All were silent. He pointed out the canvas boots that the protagonist of the film, Maryutka, was wearing. "These shots are false because her boots didn't exist during the revolution. They appeared only in 1943."

"It's a minor error," a student said.

"In our work, no errors should occur," retorted the teacher. He had a very serious attitude about such trifles that led to serious failures.

In another case, we were talking about scenes shot in slow motion. The professor explained that this technique made viewers think and feel that they were in a dream and floating, feeling very free and happy. When he was a child, he said, he one time dreamed of a flying horse carrying a rider. Dovzhenko embodied that childhood dream in his directorial work.

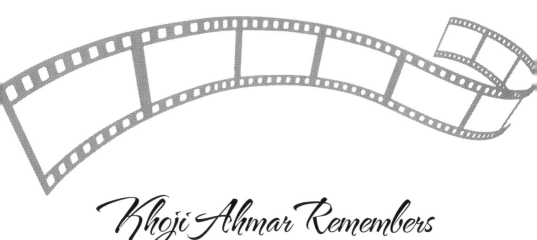

Khoji Ahmar Remembers

One day during lectures given by Dovzhenko, we heard a noise in the corridor. The professor went into the corridor and saw an electrician at work. After talking with him, Dovzhenko returned to the classroom lecture and tried to continue, but the noise resumed. He spoke to the electrician again, but the noise continued. He then put on his coat and left the institute. I ran after him. He was walking slowly with his hat in his hand. He told me that the noise had disturbed the learning process. He saw that I was shivering, and he told me to go back inside.

But I did not want to leave him alone. I asked him, "When will your car arrive?" It was supposed to come much later, after he had finished his lecture. I waved at a taxi to take him to his hotel. Alexander Petrovich did not want to go; with obvious reluctance, he slammed the taxi door.

Mosfilm offered a two-year refresher course for students who had graduated from college and had experience in any branch of art. Khoji Aka wanted to ask Dovzhenko's advice about his taking the course, so he went to his house, and the two talked for three hours about the course and a script my uncle was working on. My uncle never forgot the time and patience Dovzhenko afforded him and considered it an invaluable contribution to his career.

Dovzhenko recalled a song from his youth: "Volshebnaya Desna. Dunay pereskochiv, da Dunay pereskochiv, kopita ne vmochiv, a ne shablya kints, ni mene molodtsova, sviaty vechir." ("The magic desna Danube skipping, skipping the Danube, hooves not wetting instead sword Kintzya or fellows not me, Holy evening.") The song reminded him of his dream about the flying horse, Pegasus.

Khoji Aka remembered the day of Dovzhenko's funeral.

> There were twenty-one at the VGIK—the first and last students of Alexander Dovzhenko. They studied for one and a half years in his classes, and Dovzhenko thought of his students as his very own children.

> Moscow Central House of Writers was full of wreaths and flowers. The students crowded at this place, expressing how they are children of seventeen different nationalities. They have become one family. They all stood beside the casket and stated, "Alexander Petrovich really considered us relatives, taught us and spoke to us as if we are his OWN, and he knew everything about all of us."

At the foot of Alexander Petrovich Dovzhenko's tomb were two apple trees that were transplanted from the park in front of the National Cinema Studio named after him.

Work

Fourth-degree student VGIK Khoji Ahmar directed his first documentary, *In Don Livestock*, which premiered at the Exhibition of Economic Achievements of the USSR.

In 1958, after he had earned a diploma, Khoji Ahmar, filmmaker, returned to his native Tashkent and started working at the Uzbek Film Studio.

A Bit of History

The Russian-Bukhara Association was created in 1924 and first produced *Uzbekgoskino* and the film studio *Shark Yulduzi* (Star of the East). At the root of Uzbek Films stood Umar Mukimov, its first director, and directors Nabi Ganiev, S. Khodzhayev, E. Khamraev, Yo'ldosh Agzamov, M. Doronin, O. Freylikh, V. Dobzhansky, and A. Dorn.

The name of the studio changed several times: from Uzbek Films to Tashkent Kinostudia during the great patriotic war, back to Uzbek Films, and then to Kamil Yarmatov. In 1959, the master of Uzbek cinema got a new studio building where along with the representatives of the older generation—K. Yarmatov, Y. Agzamov, and M. Krasnyansky—began life as a creative activity of young directors, one of whom was Khoji Ahmar.

The first feature film on which he worked was *Daughter of the Ganges*; it was based on *Typhoon*, a novel by Rabindranath Tagore that was dedicated to changing India's old ways of life and the gross violations of women's rights and freedoms. The writer dreamed of his people in the future. The screenplay was written by Alexander Ginzburg; the film depicts a disastrous typhoon and how it affected people.

Rabindranath Tagore instills in the hearts of readers the hope that the people of India will wake up and renounce their dark superstitions and backward traditions. He looked at the world with new hope and had confidence in a bright future. The epilogue of the novel reads, "Our prophet said that a true Muslim is one whose words and actions do not hurt anyone. I started to recognize the voice of inner humanity in his words."

The film stars talented actors Yakub Akhmedov, Hamza Umarov, Obid Jalilov, Zaynab Sadrieva, and Maryam Yakubova. The main character, Kamola Khoji Aka, was looking for the right girl. The heroine of the novel was seventeen. He met Adiba Arifhanova in the neighboring housing complex not far from our house. The role of the nine-year-old, Umesh, played by Simon Chungak (Simon Morduhayev), was handled very professionally. This film was a hit.

Khoji Ahmar made films based on scripts he wrote, including *Hard Way* (1962), *The Swallows Arrive in Spring* (1975), *The Four Seasons* (1976), *Integral* (1970), and *Satellite of the Planet Uranus* (1990). Among his documentaries were *My Dear Muscovites, Songs of Tamara Khanum, Cooperative Resort, The Tradition of Centuries, Next on the Ground*, and *Most Obedient*. Consisting of three short stories, *The Swallows Arrive in Spring* deals with the respect all should have for nature and all living things in our forests, mountains, and fields.

The Hard Way, written by S. Nuriddinov, dealt with the everyday work of employees in the design department of the Scientific Research Institute of Agriculture. N. Kasimov, A. Rustamov, S. Azamatova, B. Nasriddinov, O. Khojaev, A. Bakirov, E. Grigorev, L. Stepanov, R. Pirmukhamedov, and G. Agzamov were among the actors.

The movie tells the story of a revolutionary breakthrough in the cotton industry, a machine that replaced hundreds of workers who formally picked cotton by hand. The first tests of the machine showed good results though the machine required some refinements. The head of the design department, Tursunov, hurried up production of the machines over the objections of others on his team.

The machines were put to work on collective farms in Uzbekistan and neighboring republics, and reports came back that the new technology did not stand up to the stress in the cotton fields. Nonetheless, the team kept working on making the machines work and ultimately succeeded. The film was a great success.

In 1960, he started working on popular movies; Khoji's documentary *Songs of Tamara Khanum* dealt with the life and work of the popular artist Tamara Artemovna Petrosyan, who performed traditional Uzbek dances and songs. During the war, she performed for soldiers, at times on the front lines. Tamara Khanum earned international recognition; she met Raj Kapoor and Dolores Ibarruri and corresponded with Charlie Chaplin, Galina Ulanova, Pablo Picasso, and Abram Khachaturian. Her ensemble performed the works of Malaev Ilyas Efraimovich, a Uzbek poet and composer. In 1986 in Tashkent, a museum was dedicated to her.

The movie *Integral* was filmed in an unusual style. The majority of the film takes place on a train. The director wanted to depict the strong will of humanity and its conscience, patience, dedication, and willingness to help others in difficult times. The assertion of this main thought is subordinated to the story of Dr. Saidov.

Here is his short retelling in the passage from the script Kh. Ahmar.

> Hunter, who was not familiar with the life and behavior of birds, built himself a tent in the high mountains and looked around to inspect the area. It was close to evening, and during this time, suddenly a large eagle began to circle the tent. This frightened the hunter, and he shot the bird without hesitation at fifty meters from him. A few times the bird tried to spread its wings, jumping, trying to fly but she couldn't. The hunter watched the struggling bird in confusion. Then another eagle swoops down to where the fallen bird lies, seizing her strong claws and picks the dead bird up, landing on the highest rock. Hunter, in confusion, thinks he should not use his gun. Hunter every morning looked over to the mountains—those birds are in the same place. On the third day he takes a jar of canned meat, and spends half a day, rising to that rock, where the birds are. The bird that was shot was lying on a rock at his feet. The hunter opens the jar and comes closer to the sitting bird, the one who took the dead bird to the rock, wanting to feed her. He was afraid to frighten her off. But the eagle proudly continues to sit back and look forward. This bird was dead too. Protecting the dead bird until his own death.

This was a story of a proud and strong bird having to deal with thoughtless and cruel humans. The film touched upon the consequences of the last war and the fate of the remaining women. Focused on the inner world of the main characters, the picture convinces viewers that if people want to be generous, they can always find ways to do so and fulfill their destinies—doing good knows no boundaries.

The cast included S. S. R. Khamza Umarov, Rustam Sagdullaev, Shukhrat Ergashev, T. Akhmedova, D. Nizamhodzhaev, R. Ibragimova, Sh. Kayumov and T. Trushina. The film was released on the eve of Dovzhenko's seventieth birthday.

One of Khoji's last works was a fantastic story, *Satellite of the Planet Uranus*, based on "Ariel," a story by A. Belyaev. Before filming began, my uncle consulted academician E. H. Turakulov, Soviet cosmonaut and twice Hero of the Soviet Union G. M. Grechko, and Hero of the Soviet Union V. V. Polyakov. The action took place in Dandorat in northern India, where teachers taught students how to levitate at a mysterious school and filled them with dreams of world domination. "If Doctor Hyde's experience peaks, then I will be able to see the Earth from an endless sky," said the protagonist, Ariel, played by Khoji Iskander Akhmar. Ariel's talents made him a weapon that greedy people wanted to use. Doctor Hyde said,

> I spoke with God Himself before proceeding to this scheme—Ariel you're one of those who are able to show the people the true path in the name that you have lived your life in solitude, your soul has always remained in the gray high contemplations and I gave you a means of communion to her, and not just to the highest ideals of the mystic, but also to the last choice of mankind.

After fleeing from the charlatan teachers, Ariel went on an incredible adventure. He interacted with cosmonauts in the United States and the Soviet Union and eventually flew to Uranus.

In *My Dear Muscovites*, Khoji Ahmar played the role of his father, and in *Satellite of the Planet Uranus*, he played the role of Kaul.

Colleagues

Honored Worker of Arts of Uzbekistan Shukhrat Abbasov wrote in his article that Khoji Ahmar's talent as a director, writer, screenwriter, and translator was limitless. In *Mountain View*, *Spring*, and *Pleasure*, he described nature so clearly and vividly that the reader saw the landscapes he clearly described.

The well-known Uzbek theater and film actor Egamberdi Musayev was preparing a show for Dovzhenko's seventieth birthday and asked his former student, Khoji Ahmar, to perform in the program. The text of the performance significantly exceeded the time limit for Khoji's presentation, and the program's host tried to cut it but did not succeed; Khoji gave a carefully thought out speech and did not miss the important details. Egamberdi Musayev speaks of Khoji Ahmar as a responsible, talented, and purposeful cultural figure.

Once, I listened to a radio reporter interviewing the actor Ulmas Alikhodzhaev, who was famous for his role as Otabek in the historical film *Past Days* directed by Yuldosh Agzamov. The novel on which the film was based was written by Abdullah Kadiri. During the conversation, a very familiar name was mentioned—Khoji Ahmar. My uncle had long since died; hearing his name mentioned was an unexpected gift to me. Ulmas Aka talked about Khoji Aka and warmly recalled his advice, which helped him become a popular actor. The talented director Khoji Ahmar sought to achieve excellence not only in his own work but also in the films of his colleagues.

In his story *The Old Man*, Khoji wrote that the inhabitants of the village Bostanlik respected Mirodil and Khoji Aka for their significant help in the construction of a bridge that reduced travel times for many who used it. When this was mentioned in Khoji's presence, he felt awkward and embarrassed but pleased that the bridge made life easier for many people.

When I was a student at the Polytechnic Institute, Rustam Mirzakarimov, a lecturer, asked me if I was related to Khoji. I told him I was, and he told me some memories he had of his friendship with my uncle during their school days. He told me how they spent free time walking together and stealing beautiful things that belonged to Khoji's older brother.

About My Parents

My father was my tutor, teacher, mentor, best friend, advocate, and consultant on legal issues. Everything I have achieved in life is because of him and my mom, Tohtahon Aya. Gulasal Ayajon and Miftah Dadajon's favorite daughter-in-law, Tohtahon Aya, was dear, kind, caring, and generous, and she took wonderful care of her big family.

As far as we know, my mother's grandfather Mirza Zhugut, or Jew as everyone called him, was very rich. He was a jeweler, and when the marriage of him and my grandmother was arranged, she betrayed three maids with her. My mom told us, and everyone was talking about it. My mother's dowry included many pieces of jewelry he had created.

Mom was kind, soft, hardworking, tactful, laconic, and hospitable. Being outwardly submissive as expected of women at the time, she really had great willpower. The first daughter-in-law of our big family, she devoted her life to us. She ironed, cleaned, cooked, and cared for us all; everything was her responsibility. During the war, she worked at a military factory, and after the war, she worked at a garment factory. Tohtahon Aya was an infinitely kindhearted woman and the true soul of our big family.

Her kindness and cordiality extended not only to the members of our family. We had dozens of relatives living with us from different regions of Uzbekistan. Many young members of related families came to Tashkent for higher education, and my mother gave them all her infinite love. She was loved and respected by all our relatives and neighbors.

Some couples live peaceful, happy, and satisfying lives while others' situations can be thorny. Young love can turn into friendship, and people living ordinary lives get used to that and do not complain. That was how it was with our parents; my mother was always busy with the household, and my father needed attention.

I was looking through our family archives and came across my father's writings about his experiences on memorable occasions in his life. Among them are these.

> I thought I had found a woman among all women, created just for me. This woman in the eyes of the people—(You) should be queen, but for him it has to be a servant, changeable as the chance of his life, fun in suffering, penetrating in trouble and in luck, and most importantly—condescending to his whims, knowing the light and its harmful flour: and in short, able not only to climb the triumphal chariot, but if necessary, and to harness it.

> Life brings us, teaches, and protects from adversity. In life, they say, nothing is forever. Yes, it is, experience shows that everything in life is incoming and outgoing …

> As time goes by, life goes on …

In the next notes, I see anxiety and excitement.

> After returning from a trip on July 30th, I felt that I was struck with a knife. My heart beat with love, my mind was preoccupied with you, I have lived by your name … I could not resist … I fell and get sick …

> At this time you was enjoying …

> No, darling, I'm not offended. I know that for you, your well-being above all else … and for you the purity, sincerity, loyalty does not exist, as there are no friendship oaths and love. There is nothing sacred to you.

> No, I'm not mad. You did what you wanted, I did what you wanted as well.

I know what you have prepared for me now the dagger, but I know even if you poke me with a needle, this will probably be the last, final and fatal …

Darling, you know how I love life, live as I appreciate someone else's life. You know what my life is connected with the life of many of my loved ones (in my family)

I know, darling, you're cruel to me exclusively, you're not worth anything to stick the dagger forth. Well, well … you've always been the queen for me, and I am your dependent …

You robbed me of everything. My pride and joy, my dreams, my future, and comfort, my happiness and my love. You took away my mind, my abilities, and my poor tormented heart …

You left me in a burning hell, and, each time pouring kerosene, insist that you are a friend that I love … Who can do that? … The most evil of the worst enemies …

You probably are very happy, so anything I wish, will be powerless front of your happiness …

But, I want you to live …

You're selfish, always looking for well-being, but finding wealth and grief. I would choose happiness and poverty …

Yes, it is very painful when you are betrayed and especially by a loved one. He continued to love, to live among his thoughts and memories, analyzing his life …

I think not everyone is able to love, and not many people have true loves. Dad had love like a bright flame. I think he was looking for a queen, but the wrong love blinded him. He lived with "a queen, queen in my heart" all his life next to him.

In recent years, he admitted that. He was the kindest father and grandfather in the world, and he was the most attentive host for visitors and friends; he was always very polite. It was impossible not to love him; not many have hearts as large as his, and he expressed that love. He wrote a proper assessment of his life and admitted his mistakes.

Find yourself as he did. See yourself and feel deeply. Listen to your inner voice, and feel and listen to your spirit, and accept it.

An Accident in Mom's Life

Gulasal Aya and my mom told me about an accident that had happened well before I was born. My mom suffered an electric shock that was so strong that she was thrown into the middle of the room. This happened due to noncompliance with safety regulations; electric irons had just appeared, and the nation was not yet accustomed to them. Prior to that, irons were heated on a coal-burning stove.

She had been badly shocked and was on the floor unconscious. No one knew what to do. Neighbors came over and made many suggestions. Someone suggested burying her in the ground, but Gulasal Ayajon was frightened and did not allow that. Uncle Muhiddin came over with his great sword, opened her clenched teeth, and pulled her tongue out. He gave her chest compressions, and in a short time, she came back to life! That memory stayed with them of course.

Uncle Muhiddin had ten children, and the youngest four were our peers with whom we frequently played. Three of them, Dilmurad, Kholmurad, and Elmurad Islamov, became famous musicians on the *doira*, a traditional Uzbek instrument. Our neighbor, well-known Gofur Azimov, taught them how to play it.

About My Sister

My older sister, Muhabbathon Opa, followed in the family tradition of teaching. After graduating from a teacher training college, she taught primary school. She then studied history at Tashkent State University and taught junior high and high school pupils. She was one of the best teachers in the area; she remains in the hearts of her students.

Everyone at school and in her mahalla respected her for her knowledge, her ability to teach, for her humanity, and for the help she would give to everyone. She also sewed for herself and for others; Muhabbathon Opa was famous for her taste and skill.

We all have favorite teachers who occupy a special place in our hearts. Muazzamhon Opa, Muhabbathon Opa, was one such teacher.

It is appropriate to recall here the poem of Omar Khayyam.

> One does not follow it than smell roses …
> Another of the mountain herbs will produce honey …
> Someone gets a trifle, forever remembers,
> Someone you give life, and he did not understand.
> To live life wisely, ought you to know a lot,
> Two important rules to remember the beginning:
> You better starve than be horrible there,
> And better be alone than with just anyone.
>
> Days of life even Bitter Exalt,
> After all, they are gone forever.

Conclusion

This is my first book, and I hope my readers will find it interesting and enjoyable. I want people to remember and appreciate the good deeds done for the sake of souls and the good of the world; we should follow the good examples of the older generation.

Before I started to write this book, I read a lot of books, listened to lectures, and searched the internet. I became interested in the biographies of great and famous people including George Washington, Emmanuel Kant, Charlie Chaplin, Grace Kelly, Galina Ulanova, Mademoiselle Chanel, Madame Rothschild, and many others. I really liked the books of Esther Hicks, Louis Hay, and especially Wayne Dyer, who wrote about people with good hearts and clean souls. I really liked Dyer's story about how willpower helped him live a happy, productive, and active life. He impressed me with a lecture in which he shared his life's observations and conclusions.

This is the case of the teaching practices of Miss Thompson, who taught grade school. She started her lessons by telling her students that she loved them all. But that was not true. One of her students, Teddy, was not tidy, was always dirty, and had no interest in school. She did not see anything attractive in this student and treated him indifferently.

But she decided to find out more about him. His first-grade teacher had written that he was intelligent and gifted. His second-grade teacher had written that his mother's illness had distracted him. His third-grade teacher had written that his mother had died and his father had begun to drink. His fourth-grade teacher said that his effort in school was at a low level and that he sometimes slept in class. His fifth-grade teacher had written that he had lost all interest in school. Miss Thompson realized that the boy was in need of attention.

On Mother's Day, her students gave her gifts, some of which they had made and some of which they had bought. Teddy gave her a dirty paper bag in which she found half a bottle of perfume and a bracelet that was missing some stones. Miss Thompson put the bracelet on, and the next day, she came to school after having put on some of the perfume. That day, Teddy told her that she smelled like his mother.

Miss Thompson and everyone else started noticing change in Teddy. He became attentive in class, and he started dressing better. He worked hard and did well in his studies. He invited Miss Thompson to his high school graduation.

He went to college, and he kept in touch with her. After he graduated from college, he wrote to her asking if she would take the place of his mother at his wedding ceremony. He signed his letter "Dr. Teddy."

They remained friends for a long time.

During a lecture, Dyer asked a girl, "If you squished an orange, what would you get?"

"Orange juice of course," she said.

He said that we would get juice out of any fruit we squeezed. What is inside would come out. He said it was the same with people. Great people will be kind, just, and generous, and if we look around us, we will see beauty.

When we are with nature, we can discover many things that we overlooked in the past because we were not paying attention, and we can change our lives if we look through different eyes. Unfortunately, we are often too busy with work, children, and chores and do not notice how time flies and the beauty around us, but it is never too late to change.

One day, a person looks in the mirror and sees himself and suddenly understands the beauty of nature in rainbows and stars and he thinks of his life—what he has done and what he has not done. That happened to me, and it prompted me to pay tribute to my family with this book. They never spared themselves for the sake of a good cause and their children's futures.

I hope my readers find some useful information in this book.

I thank my uncle Kudrat Akhmerov; Miradil Akhmerov for his record and captured experiences; their sisters Mukarramhon Aliyeva, Muazzamhon Akhmerova, and brother Khabibulla Akhmerov for saving my father's notes; and nephew Shakhrukh Khamraliev for documents and photos he sent me.

I thank everyone who shared with me their priceless photos and good memories. I end my story with a poem by Omar Khayyam.

> Since we only live one moment in the world,
> Live merrily—let happiness guide you.
> Communicate with the sage and know that our body is
> Only dust and drop, spark and wind.
>
> The purpose and crown of His creation is—us,
> The peak of thought is a moment of insight—we.
> The circle of the universe is a—precious ring,
> It has the best stone, no doubt—we are.

1956-57. Actors, working team and Khoji Ahmar, when they were working on a movie called "Daughter of Ganges"

На съемках фильма "Интеграл"

Behind the scenes of the film "Integral"

Khoji Ahmar in an editing studio

1955-56. Moscow. Student years in Soviet State
Institute of Cinematography (VGIK)

Tamarahanum

Tamarahanum

Ulmas Alikhojaev footage from Past Days

Khoji Ahmar footage from
"Satellite of The Planet Uranus", his role as Kaul

Khoji Ahmar on the cover of Cinema magazine

1954. Kibray. Members of United Writers of Uzbekistan at a picnic.

Khoji Ahmar and others working on the movie "Hard Way".

1987. At the Cinema House. Presentation of a
movie "Satellite of Planet Uranus"

1987. My Father and my kids.

Newspaper article about Kh.Aliev.

My cousin Izzat and his wife Mehrigul and their kids Zaina,
Adina, Zamir, and my Granddaughter Shirina.

At the wedding party: My sister Lolabanu, my Aunthy Mukarramhon
Opa, Gulyahon Opa, Muzzamhon Opa and her grandson Mirabror.

1973. Chimgan. My student years working in a pioneer camp and my class members, along with the teacher in the middle.

Miradil Ahmerov

Miradil Ahmerov

My dad and me. Moskow, Red Square, August, 1976

Kudrat Aka and his family.

2019. November. Washington. Home.
Muazzamhon Opa and me.

2013. Orlando. My son Farruh and Daughter Gulruhbanu

My son Farruh and Daughter Gulruhbanu

1971. Chirchik. In the middle Grandpa,
behind him Dad visiting Family relatives

My mom Tohtahon Aya at work

Tohtahon Aya

1960. Tashkent, Garment factory 2.
My mom and her friend.

1960. Tashkent. Home. Me and Dilmurad Islamov

1961. Tashkent. Parents house. My mom and my
aunties. (Mom visiting her sisters)

Me.

Gulasal Ahmerova

Muazzam Ahmerova

Muhabbat Ahmerova (Shayakubova)

Miftah Dadajon, Gulasal Ayajon and Kudrat
Aka, Moskow, Summer time, 1961

Mukarram Ahmerova (Alieva)

From the left: Mirolim, Hurshidahon, Miraziz, Jahongir, Muazzamhon Opa, Kudrat Aka, Gulyahon Opa, Mukarramhon Opa and her daughter Malikahon, Ruhsora, Mohinur,Nigorahon, Kamila, Mirabror on the weekend visiting uncle. Grandparents house.

Home. 1987. Our family. In the middle parents around kids and grandkids.

Home. 1987. Father.

Moskow. 1955. Khoji Ahmar behind him his brother Miradil and students of VGIK.

Home. 1980. Gulasal Aya and Daddy.

Front of apartment. 1988. Spring.
Daddy with grandchildren

Khoji Ahmar.

M.Chimgan. 2003. Summer. Brother Habibulla his
wife Svetlana and daughter Kamiilla.

Moskow. 1956. Brothers: Khoji Aka,
Kudrat Aka and his friend.

Moscow. 1955. Khoji Aka,
Daddy and student from Check republic

Front of Khoji Aka's home.1985. May. Wedding party.

Moscow. 1956. Khoji Aka,
Daddy and ankle Mahmudjon Aka

Moscow. 1957. USSR Exebition.
Gulasal Aya and Daddy.

Tashkent. 1960. Khoji Ahmar in role.

Home of Kh.Aliev. 1971. Me and Khaybat Aka's
Daughter Malika and Son Nodir

Tashkent. 1971. Home.
Khaybat Aka, his Family, Muazzam Opa and me.

Moscow. 1956. Red Square. Miftah Dadajon.

Tashkent. 1952. Home in the yard.
My sister Muhabbathon Opa.

Tashkent. 1963. Home in the yard.
My sister Lolabanu and brother Khabib.

Moscow. 1971. Kremlin Tsar Bell.
Khoji Aka and his Mom.

Georgia. 1970. Gory.
Daddy visiting Home of I.V. Stalin.

Tashkent. 1987. Home.
Me and my kids: Gulruh and Farruh

Gulistan. 1971. November 7 After Demonstration.
From right second Daddy and his colleagues.

Tashkent. 1964. Home.
Khoji Aka and his Son.

Moscow. 1960. Red Square.
Daddy and his ankle Mahmudjon Aka.

Tashkent. 1932. Tohtahon Aya in the middle
and her cousins: Jamilya and Nazira

Tashkent. 1971. Mother of Khaybat
aka- Muazzamhon Aya.

Lenigrad. 1971.
Khoji Aka, his Mom and son.

About the Author

I was born prematurely, and I weighed only two kilograms. No one thought I would survive, so my parents didn't give me a name for a month. Mom was so worried about me that she would not leave the house. But when Khoji Aka came back from Moscow on vacation, he gave me a name, got my birth certificate, and told my mother that I would live.

How funny!

I graduated from the Faculty of Chemical Technology at the Tashkent Polytechnic Institute in 1977 and started working for the Central Asian Research Institute. I actively worked in the Komsomol organization after I was transferred to an elected post.

From 1993 to 1999, I was the deputy head of the Secretariat and head of the office at the Ministry of Foreign Affairs of Uzbekistan.

I have loved children all my life. While studying at the institute, I spent all five years and three seasons at a pioneer camp working as a pioneer courier.

I like to sew; it's a talent I inherited from my mother. I sew and embroider for my soul's sake. As you can see, sometimes I write. This book is my first. In it, I write mainly about the life and work of the famous film director Khoji Ahmar. I thoughtfully and scrupulously conducted research and interviewed relatives, friends, and acquaintances. This book also contains what I have learned about our large family and my beautiful, beloved, and dear people and their values, loves, relationships, tireless activity, successes, and achievements. Writing has always intrigued me, so here's my shot at it.

I have a daughter and a son and grandkids who were born in the United States. I love them all very much.

Printed in the United States
by Baker & Taylor Publisher Services